Who Are "They" Anyway?

A TALE OF ACHIEVING SUCCESS AT WORK
THROUGH PERSONAL ACCOUNTABILITY

BJ Gallagher

and Steve Ventura

Dearborn™
Trade Publishing
A **Kaplan Professional** Company

Vice President and Publisher: Cynthia A. Zigmund
Acquisitions Editor: Jonathan Malysiak
Senior Managing Editor: Jack Kiburz
Interior Design: Lucy Jenkins
Cover Design: Design Solutions
Typesetting: Elizabeth Pitts

© 2004 by BJ Gallagher

Published by Dearborn Trade Publishing
A Kaplan Professional Company

04 05 06 10 9 8 7 6 5 4 3 2 1

Library of Congress Cataloging-in-Publication Data

Hateley, B. J. Gallagher (Barbara J. Gallagher), 1949-
  Who are "they" anyway? : a tale of achieving success at work through personal accountability / by B.J. Gallagher & Steve Ventura.
    p. cm.
  Includes bibliographical references.
  ISBN 0-7931-8829-6 (hb.)
  1. Performance standards. 2. Responsibility. 3. Personnel management. 4. Job satisfaction. 5. Employees—Attitudes. I. Ventura, Steve. II. Title.
HF5549.5.P35H38   2004
650.1—dc22

2004004601

Praise for *Who Are "They" Anyway?*

"A good story is like a good sermon—it should both teach and inspire. This book does both beautifully. I found myself nodding in agreement as I read it. I recognize the characters and the situations—all so familiar. The story ends with an important discovery and a surprising twist that brought a smile to my face."

—**Warren Bennis,** Distinguished Professor of Business Administration at the University of Southern California, and author of *On Becoming a Leader* and *Geeks and Geezers: How Era, Values and Defining Moments Shape Leaders*

"Who Are 'They' Anyway? represents a go-to source for driving accountability in your organization by compelling readers to look at the power of 'me' versus 'they.'"

—**David C. Novak,** Chairman and CEO of Yum! Brands, Inc. (KFC, Taco Bell, Pizza Hut, A&W, Long John Silver's)

"People forget facts and figures, but they remember stories. That's why I love this book—it makes an important point in a way that you won't forget. The first part of the book is a parable about one man's search for someone to solve his problems at work. The second part is where 'the rubber meets the road,' as we get the opportunity to apply the lessons of the story to ourselves. This is storytelling at its best—both inspiring and practical!"

—**Ann Rhoades,** President of People Ink, former EVP of People for JetBlue Airways, former EVP of Human Resources for Doubletree Hotels Corporation, and former VP of People for Southwest Airlines

"Great truths are often best conveyed in stories and parables. This book is a luminous pearl of wisdom—conveying a great truth for all of us, no matter where we work. Personal responsibility is essential not just in business, but also in churches and synagogues, colleges and universities, the government and the military, hospitals, schools, and nonprofit organizations —anywhere that people are working together for a common purpose."

—**Craig Neal,** Cofounder, the Heartland Institute

"Truth, like the wind, can caress us with gentle breezes that wisp across our face. Truth, like the wind, can sweep us off our feet with the strength of its mighty gales. *Who Are 'They' Anyway?* is truth that gently caresses our spirits with wisps of humor and forcefully sweeps us off our feet with gales of wisdom. *Who Are 'They' Anyway?* like the wind, surrounds us, moves us, presses against our spirits, permeates our pain, our emotion, our comfort, our business, our religion, our lives, our very existence. Like the wind, *Who Are 'They' Anyway?* is gentle and mighty! It is truth!"

—**Rev. Cecil Murray,** Senior Minister,
First African Methodist Episcopal Church

"If you've ever felt like a victim or ever helped another who felt like a victim, this book will give you the wisdom, chutzpah, and methods to change being a prey into being a champ."

—**Chip R. Bell,** author of *Magnetic Service*

"BJ and Steve teach a valuable lesson about responsibility through their parable, and then amplify the teachings beautifully in their toolkit. Thanks, BJ and Steve! You took an all-too-common, counterproductive habit and confronted us with it in an engaging and memorable way!"

—**Beverly Kaye,** coauthor of *Love It, Don't Leave It: 26 Ways to Get What You Want at Work,* as well as the bestseller *Love 'Em or Lose 'Em: Getting Good People to Stay*

Dedication

For Our Dads,
Ken Gallagher and Antonio Ventura.
You are the most important men in our lives.
You taught us much about responsibility,
achievement, hard work, success, and
how great it feels to take initiative and take action.
Thanks, Dad.

Contents

PART THREE

Additional Resources

Foreword

Do people in your organization act like victims—blaming everyone and everything else for their problems? Are employees and managers caught up in the blame game of finger-pointing and defensiveness?

Unfortunately, this game is played every day in organizations both large and small—the result is lower productivity, poor teamwork, resentment and grudges, and terrible morale. Employees blame management for their problems; managers are frustrated and blame employees for not taking initiative; and departments blame other departments whenever things go wrong. A climate of accusation and retribution becomes pervasive. Everyone thinks it's someone else's job to do something!

What's the answer? Personal responsibility. Only when employees and managers alike take initiative and become accountable for their *own* behaviors and results, can things change. This wonderful book by BJ Gallagher and Steve Ventura gives us the opportunity to begin that change—within ourselves and within our organizations.

Part One is the story of an average Joe who goes in search of the ephemeral "they," who everyone seems to think is responsible for making things better. Part Two gives us the opportunity to apply the moral of the story to our own work lives. We move from parable to practice with thought-provoking quizzes and self-assessments that encourage us to reflect on our own level of personal responsibility and willingness to take initiative. Short essays stimulate our thinking about how we might become more successful by making a few changes in the way we approach situations and problems at work. And inspiring quotes from accomplished people encourage us to rise to the occasion and become more powerful in how we live our lives. Altogether, the parable and the experiential exercises provide a terrific learning experience for team members and managers alike.

A one-minute praising to Steve Ventura for teaming up with BJ Gallagher—I'm a big BJ Gallagher fan, and together they are teaching us an important lesson in such an enlightening and entertaining way!

—Ken Blanchard, coauthor of *The One Minute Manager*® and *The On-Time, On-Target Manager*

PART ONE

The Story

This is the story
of a person who has a problem.

Who is he?

Just a regular guy,
*   in a regular job,*
*   in a regular organization.*

What kind of a problem?

Well, let's just say
it's one that's not at all
uncommon . . .

. . . perhaps you've even had it yourself.

See if his story
*   sounds familiar . . .*

For many years
I've heard about "they". . .
    and I've often wondered
    just who are *they,* anyway?

You know who I'm talking about:

> *They could have prevented this situation.*
> *They never tell us what's really going on.*
> *They oughta DO something about this!*
> *It's their fault!*

I'm sure you've heard this, too:

> *They don't care about quality and service;*
> *it's all about numbers and the bottom line.*
> *They're never around when you need them,*
> *you know.*
> *They can't decide what they want us to do.*
> *They do just enough to get by.*
> *When are they gonna learn?*

They're everywhere,
I swear!

Just listen to people complain:

> *They're ruining this organization.*
> *They're driving me crazy!*
> *They never listen.*
> *They can't be trusted.*
> *They're only out for themselves.*
> *They're never satisfied.*
> *They could solve our problems if they really*
> *wanted to.*
> *I'm tired of them not pulling their share*
> *of the load!*

It's downright disconcerting.

They're in charge of everything,
  but they don't tell us anything.
They make the rules and policies
  by which we must work,
    but those rules and policies
      often get in the way of our work.

They tell us
  we need to *embrace* change,
    but they don't change themselves.
They seem to have all the power,
  but they don't use it wisely.

They want,
  they expect,
    they demand,
they cut,
  they control,
    they command,
they, they, they . . .

It's always about "they"!

Just who are THEY, anyway?

Now, don't get me wrong . . .
    I like my job.
And the organization's
    not bad,
        as organizations go.

I like the people here,
    some are really great,
and the members of my team,
    well, we get along OK.

But, it's so hard
to deal with problems sometimes . . .

And worse yet,
    it's impossible to try
    to change anything,
because they won't let us—
they won't approve it;
    they say the economy is iffy,
        so better not take a risk.

Why, just recently,
I encountered a problem
with this new technology
we're supposed to be
implementing.

I followed the procedures,
        did what I'd learned
        in the training,
                but the problem persisted.

I took my troubles to my teammates,
    but they offered little in the way of help . . .

One said,
"I don't know.
Read the manual
they gave you."

Another replied,
"Don't ask me,
that new stuff was *their* idea,
not mine."

And a third just shrugged
and shuffled away.

So I went to ask my boss.

Her door was open,
        so I walked right in.
She looked up from the paperwork
        on her desk.
"What's up?"
        she asked,
as she motioned for me to sit.

"What's up is my frustration,"
        I replied.
"I try to do a good job,
but problems come up,
some of which
could have been prevented.
But when I talk to others
all I hear is:
        They don't want to hear about problems.
        They only want good news.
        They don't like people who rock the boat.
And me, I'm trying to figure out
who this 'THEY' is!

"You're my boss . . .
Are *you* one of *'them'*?
Are *you* responsible?"

My boss leaned back
        in her chair
                as she said,
"Don't I wish!
If I were one of them,
things would be
a lot different around here.
But they haven't seen fit
to include me in their group.
Like you, I just work here."

"Well, then,"
        I asked,
"Can you tell me
who *they* are . . .
        and where I can find *them?*"

"You know,"
        she replied,
"They're the guys who run this place—
the people who make
the daily decisions.
They're always in charge.
Go upstairs
where the senior managers work.
I'm pretty sure
that's where *they* are."

So upstairs I went,
　　　hopeful that *they*
　　　would be there.

I asked the receptionist,
"Are they in?
I need to see them.
We've got problems
that need fixing."

"They? Here?"
　　　she responded.
"You must be mistaken.
There's no one here
but us,
and we're certainly not responsible
for the problems you describe.
They're at headquarters—
those who you seek—
in that tall building
downtown."

So downtown I went,
        reasonably certain
        that they would be there.

Which building?
I wondered
        when I arrived,
looking up at
        all the skyscrapers so tall—
                all looking alike.

Surely the people responsible
        are in one of these buildings.
But which one?
I'll ask someone . . .

"Excuse me, sir,
I'm looking for 'them'—do you know
where they are?"

"Of course I do—everyone knows
where *they* are."
     He frowned at me
     as he set his briefcase down.
"They're in the Boardroom,
up there on the 47th floor."
     He pointed to the top
     of the tallest building.
"When you find them,
tell them to shape up.
There are problems
that need taking care of
and people
who need their attention."

"I'll tell them,"
    I replied.
"Thank you
for your directions . . . "

But I don't think he heard me.

For just then
the traffic light changed,
    and the waiting crowd
    surged across
    the intersection.

So I shrugged good-bye
and headed for the elevator
    in the tallest building—
    relentless in my search for *them*.

When I reached the top,
    the elevator doors opened,
      and a crowd of suits
      was standing there.
The meeting had just adjourned,
    and everyone was gathered,
      waiting for the elevator.

"Excuse me,
are you the people in charge?
I've been looking for you
everywhere."

"Heck, no,"
    one suit replied,
"But I'd sure like to give *them*
a piece of my mind!"

His face turned red
as he continued,
"They're in their union hall.
Everyone knows
it's Labor that controls
what happens around here."

"Yeah,
those guys are tough cookies!"
    another suit chimed in.
"We've tried to get them
to step up to the plate
and deal
with our concerns.
It's like speaking
to a stone wall.
I doubt that talking
will do you any good—
at least not with *them*."

"Well,
I've got to try,"
    I replied.
"There are problems
that need attention.
Success is at stake . . .
our jobs are at stake!
And *they* need
to do something!
Don't you see?
I've got to continue
my search for *them*."

So, down to the union hall
I taxied,
      hoping that
      it wasn't too late
      already.

The taxi driver
was gruff
but friendly.
"You in town
on business or pleasure?"
      he asked,
peering at me
in his rearview mirror.

"Business,"
      I replied.
"Serious business."

"Yeah?"
      he replied,
      an eyebrow raised.

"Yeah,"
      I nodded,
"I'm hoping soon
to talk to *them*."

"Good luck!"
    he snorted
        sarcastically.
"Pretty hopeless,
if you ask me."

"Well, you're not alone
in feeling that way,"
    I sighed.
"A lot of people
feel the same.
But nonetheless,
I must go on.
I can't stop now—I've come too far."

"OK then, here we are,"
    as he pulled to the curb
        in front of
            a redbrick building.

"That'll be twelve-fifty,"
    he said.

I handed him
    his fare
        and a generous tip
            and waved as he drove away.

I tried not to think
    that maybe he was right.

I turned to face the building.
"I sure hope they're here—
I'm getting tired of looking."

Once inside
I paused—
uncertain which office to try.

"Can I help ya?"
        a voice came from behind me.

"You bet,"
        I smiled,
        turning to face
        the man in shirtsleeves.
"I was told that I could find
them here."

"What 'them'
would that be?"
        he asked.

"The ones responsible
for what happens
at work,"
        I answered.
"I was told that
they're here."

"Ha!
Who the heck
told you that?"
        he laughed,
                taking the cigar
                        out of his mouth.
"Whoever it was
fed you a bunch of bull!"

He slapped me on the shoulder
as if we were sharing a joke.
Shaking his head
he continued,
"It's those bean counters—
that's who you should be talking to.
Those Finance guys—
they're the ones who call the shots.
They run everything by the numbers.
It's the guys with the calculators
you're looking for."

"Where will I find them?"
        I asked
                as he turned to walk away.

"Just follow the money . . . "
        came his reply,
                before he disappeared
                        down the hall.

Disappointed
    and dejected,
I turned slowly
    to walk outside.

"This is taking
a lot longer
than I thought,"
    I mumbled
    to no one in particular.
"Who *are* the people
responsible
for what happens here?
I don't have forever
to find them.
Things aren't getting any better,
and *they* need to DO something!"

I headed back downtown—
    still on my quest—
        still in search of *them*.

I arrived at a building
all glass and chrome,
and pushed my way
through the revolving door
and followed the signs
to the Finance Department.

"Excuse me, miss,"
    I inquired at the information desk,
"I was directed here
to meet with *them*—
can you let *them* know I'm here?"

"Oh . . . uh . . . I'm sorry,
you've been misdirected,"
    she smiled sweetly.
"They're not here—
we just crunch numbers,
that's all we do."

"But isn't this
where the Controller works?
And isn't he or she *in control?*"
    I asked.

"Well, yes,"
    she answered,
"This is where the Controller works,
but she doesn't really *control* things.
They do!"

"Then where on earth
can I find *them*?!"
    I almost shouted,
        losing my cool.
"We've got problems,
and issues,
and concerns,
and nothing will ever get fixed
if I can't find
this *'they'* who are responsible!"

"Well, don't take it out on me,"
    she snipped,
        rightly taken aback
           by my outburst.

"I'm sorry,
I'm so sorry,"
        I hastened to say.
"I'm not angry with you;
I'm just tired of looking
here, there, and everywhere.
Please accept my apology."

"Of course,"
        she replied,
"I know how you feel.
They can be pretty upsetting,
can't they?
Have a seat
and I'll call
Human Resources
and see if they
can help you,
OK?"

What could I say?
At this point,
        I was about ready to give up.
"Sure," I sighed
        as I dropped into
        a big leather chair.

As I sat there
        cooling my heels,
I noticed a copy
of our organization's annual report
        on the table
                beside me.
I picked it up
        and started
                thumbing through it.

Our workplace looked so rosy
        depicted on
                the slick pages . . .
smiling employees
        of all colors and hues,
dignified executives
        exuding power and confidence
                from their pinstripes.
And teamwork—
        above all, teamwork—
                emphasized on
                        page after page.

"One big happy family . . . "
        I muttered to myself,
". . . yeah, right."
Frustration
and cynicism
welled up
in my throat.

Just then,
a cheery woman
from Human Resources
walked in.
"I understand
you're having a problem,"
        she said in her
                most soothing voice.
"I'm so sorry.
Is there anything
I can do to help?"

"I don't know,"
        I replied wearily.
"Maybe it's hopeless.
I've been trying
to find the 'they'
that I hear
people talking about
all the time.

"My teammates
complain about 'they';
        my boss grumbles
        about 'they';
                and people I talk to
                in other departments
                bemoan all the problems
                        caused by this
                        mysterious and elusive *'they.'*

"I'm just trying to find out,
who are *they,*
anyway?"

"I know just what you mean,"
        she nodded
                sympathetically.

"It's my understanding
that *they* are all
in the *Line* departments . . .
you know, Operations.
I'm in HR,
and we're just a
Staff department,
no power or
authority.
We, too, are frustrated
with *them*,
but there's nothing
we can do.
It's just the way things are."

I didn't reply.
I just sat there,
taking in
what she had said.

I was out of steam,
no longer angry,
just resigned.

"Well, thank you
for your time,"
        I said,
                getting up
                from my chair.
I extended my hand
        and she
                shook it graciously.

"I wish I could be
of more help,"
        she smiled,
                a bit sadly.

"Oh, it's OK,"
        I said,
"At this point
I don't think *anyone*
can help.
It doesn't appear that
anyone is responsible
for *anything*!

"I think I'll just go
to the cafeteria
and get a cup of coffee."

We walked down the hall
        together,
                silently.

"I'm going to stop
at the rest room here
and wash my hands,"
          I told her.
"Thanks again for your time."

"Sure, anytime,"
          she waved
                    as she continued
                              down the hall.
"See ya."

I pushed open
        the bathroom door
                and walked in.

The place
        was empty
except for one guy
        washing his hands
                at one of the sinks.

I went to another sink
        and turned on the faucet.

"Nice day, isn't it?"
        he observed.

"Not particularly,"
        came my glum reply.

"Gotta problem?"
        he queried.

I looked over
        at him.
I didn't recognize him,
        but that
        didn't mean anything—
                it's a big organization.

"Oh, I don't wanna
bore you
with all the gory details.
Let's just say
I'm havin' a bad day."

"Yeah?"
　　　his raised eyebrows
　　　　　　continued to query.

"Yeah,"
　　　I replied,
"I've spent all day
trying to find out
who's really in charge here . . .
Who's responsible
when things go wrong?
Who's responsible
for solving problems?
Who's responsible
for making a difference?"

"Oh, I see,"
　　　he answered.

"I just wanna know
who are *they*, anyway?"
　　　I blurted
　　　　　　in frustration.

"Oh, yeah,
that's a good one,"
        he nodded.
"I've struggled with
the very same question
myself."

"Right.
But *nobody's* got
the answer,"
        I complained.
"I've been all over
the place,
and I came up
empty-handed.
Nothing.
Zip.
Nada.
Zero."

"Ya don't say,"
        he replied
                with a touch
                        of bemusement
                                in his voice.

I shot him a glance—
"You know somethin'
I don't know?"

"Not really,"
        he said.
"I just know
that sometimes
people look for answers
in every place
except the most obvious one.

"Haven't you had
that experience?
You spend all day
lookin' for something—
till finally
you give up
in frustration.

"And once you give up,
suddenly
what you're looking for
shows up—
right in plain sight,
right under your nose!"

"Well, yeah," I agreed,
"I *have* had that experience . . .
looking for car keys,
the TV remote,
the leash for the dog.
Yup,
sometimes it *is* right there
under my nose."

"Well, perhaps
that's what's happening here.
Could be that
your answer is
hiding in plain sight,"
       he said,
             as he wiped his hands
             with paper towels.

"Well, I see
what you're saying,"
        I countered.
"But, I don't think
it applies in this situation."

"Hmmm,
maybe so, maybe not,"
        he said,
                as he headed
                        for the door.
"It was just a thought."

"Well,
thanks anyway . . . "
        I said lamely.

Too late.
He was gone.

"Huh?"
I said to myself.
"Hiding in plain sight . . .
that can't be . . . "

Now alone,
I turned on the water,
leaned over the sink,
and began washing my hands—
washing them of this whole matter,
this futile search.

I turned up the hot water
    and bent further
        to splash some water
        on my face.
This whole ordeal
    had been exhausting,
and I hoped I could wash the fatigue
    from my face.

The hot water felt good . . .
    soothing,
        relaxing,
            calming.

I took my time . . .
    cupping the running water
    in my hands
        and bringing it
        to my face.
Ahhh . . .

Finally,
I straightened up,
        grabbed some paper towels
        from the dispenser,
                and began to dry my face.
As I watched myself
        in the slightly steamy mirror,
my mind kept repeating
        the stranger's words . . .

'Hiding in plain sight
        right under my nose . . . '

Then suddenly
it dawned on me—
as if someone
had flipped a switch
in my mind:
"Ha!
There's the answer—
      right in the mirror
            looking back at me!
"It's as plain
      as the nose on my face.
The answer is ME!"

"Well,
       whaddya know?
I've been looking for
       responsibility
          in all the wrong places!

"I thought someone *else*
       was accountable—
I thought that *they* must have
       the answers.

"Now at last I see—
       there is no they . . .
          there is only ME."

I tossed the paper towel
        in the trash
and headed for the door.
In a moment of impulse,
I turned back to the mirror,
        still a little steamy
        from the hot water.

As I had sometimes done
        as a child,
I used my finger
        to write on
                the slightly foggy mirror—
ME
        in big block letters.

I stood back and smiled.

Just then,
someone else
came into the washroom.

Glancing at me,
        then at the mirror,
                then back to me,
                        he looked puzzled.
"What's that?"
        he asked.

"I just solved a problem
        I was working on,"
                I answered.
"I discovered
        that I had the solution
                all along . . .
I just didn't know it."

"Really?"
he mused
as he looked
at ME in the mirror.

I told him briefly
of my frustrating day
and my fruitless search
for *they*.

"That's quite a tale,"
    he said
    as he ran a comb through his hair.
"And I definitely think
you've got
a right answer."

"Thanks,"
I replied.

"And maybe there's more . . . "
    he continued.

"More what?"
    I asked.

"More right answers.
Like many questions
    in life,
there may even be
more than one
right answer
to your question,"
    he said.

"Yes,
perhaps
you're right,"
    I agreed.

"Here's another possibility,"
    he said,
as he wrote
on the steamy mirror:

WE

"Hey, you're right,"
    I chuckled.
"I never thought of that."

"Well,"
he replied,
"what's that old saying,
'Two heads
are better than one' . . . ?
I guess it's true."

"Yeah,"
        I nodded,
"and as I look at the two words,
I notice that they look kinda like
two sides of the same coin . . .
        See?
If you put ME here,
and WE right below it,
it looks like
they are mirroring each other.

ME
WE

"WE and ME go together,
        like a right and left hand
                working together."

"I like the way you think!"
        he exclaimed
as we both stood looking
        at the words.

We saw our words,
and we saw our faces,
        reflected together in the mirror.

"Reminds me of that
      fairy tale
I used to read to my daughter
      when she was little . . .

but as I look at this, what
comes to mind is:
      Mirror, mirror, on the wall,
      who's responsible after all?

"ME," I said.

"And WE," he said.

We both fell silent for a moment . . .

"Well, I gotta run,"
  I broke the silence,
    heading for the door.

"What's your hurry?"
  he asked
  as he followed me.

"No time to waste . . .
I've got things to do
and problems to solve!"
  I replied.

"Hey, so do I!"
  he nodded
    in agreement.

And we walked out
  through the doorway
    together.

THE END . . . ?

No, It's Just the Beginning

PART TWO

From Parable to Practice

ME

WE

Did you recognize any of the people in the story? Were the situations familiar? More important, did you recognize *yourself* in the story?

This next section is designed to help you think about and talk about how much responsibility and initiative you take at work. It's an opportunity to assess how others act in your organization, and to reflect on your own actions as well. You can analyze the way you approach problems. Do you want to take more personal responsibility? What do you have to gain? What do you have to lose?

In short, what follows is a personal toolkit designed to help you reflect on the parable and apply the key lessons to your own work. You can have a conversation with yourself about your own job/career/ future. You can make choices about how you may want to try doing things a little differently in the future. The choice is always yours. We simply offer alternatives and options. There are no "shoulds" here—only "coulds."

"My interest is in the future, because I'm going to spend the rest of my life there."

C. F. KETTERING, *automotive engineer and inventor*

"There is no *try* . . . there is only *do*."

YODA, *in* Star Wars *(George Lucas)*

Do People in Your Organization Exercise Initiative and Take Responsibility?

In our story, we saw an entire organization in which everyone thought that someone else was the problem—that someone else must have the solution. This kind of pervasive blame game was deeply ingrained in their corporate culture. How would you assess the culture where *you* work?

YES NO

___ ___ 1. Do people refer to "they" or "them" when talking about management or other departments? ("They won't let us . . . ," "They keep us in the dark . . . ," "They spend all the money, but we do all the work," etc.)

___ ___ 2. Are people often worried about "covering their backsides" ("CYA") with documentation, approvals, etc.? ("I called him with the information, but also wrote him a memo for CYA purposes.")

___ ___ 3. Do employees feel like "victims" of management? Do they talk and act like they're helpless and have no control?

___ ___ 4. Do some individuals take all the credit for other people's ideas or for group accomplishments?

5. Are people quick to point out how they're not at fault when something goes wrong?

6. Do you frequently hear people whining and complaining about all the many reasons why they *can't* do what needs to be done?

7. Do you hear people say, "That's not my job"?

8. Do supervisors and managers often express frustration that "employees don't take initiative"?

9. Are people pointing out and complaining about problems all the time but rarely proposing solutions?

10. Do people hide behind policies and procedures, job descriptions, employee handbooks, etc., when justifying why they can't do certain things?

TOTALS

> "Man must cease attributing his problems to his environment, and learn to exercise his will—his personal responsibility."
>
> **ALBERT SCHWEITZER**, *French physician, philosopher, humanitarian, and Nobel prize recipient*

SCORING:

LOWEST SCORE: If you answered **"NO" to all ten** of these questions, congratulations! You work in an organization with a high level of personal accountability. Managers and employees alike take responsibility for initiating ideas and resolving problems when they occur.

LOW SCORE: If you answered **"YES" to three or fewer** of these questions, your organization is in pretty good shape. In general, most people feel accountable and take responsibility for improving organizational performance. Only occasionally does the blame game occur.

MODERATE SCORE: If you answered **"YES" on four to six** of these questions, you have cause for concern. Employees are quick to point fingers of blame and slow to accept responsibility for finding solutions. There is probably a fairly high level of fear present, and people are punished for taking initiative outside their job descriptions or for bending the rules. Some people really feel like "victims."

HIGH SCORE: If you answered **"YES" to seven or more** of these questions, your organization has reached the major leagues of playing the blame game! Employees feel like victims of management; management feels like victims because employees "won't take initiative"; and *everyone* is expending a great deal of energy blaming everyone else. Your organization has some serious work ahead if it wants to establish a culture of accountability.

"... marketing blames R&D for designing products or features the customer doesn't need instead of the ones marketing knows the customer wants; sales attacks marketing for such inadequate support as ill-conceived brochures or mistargeted commercials; manufacturing accuses sales of signing off on poor forecasts that cause either too many back orders or too much inventory; R&D points the finger at manufacturing for not resolving manufacturability... problems on the factory floor; vice presidents heap scorn on directors for not taking more responsibility, while directors chide vice presidents for either not providing sufficient guidelines or not letting go. Around and around it goes, a merry-go-round of accusations that does nothing to solve an organization's problems."

—Roger Connors, Tom Smith, and Craig Hickman,
authors of *The Oz Principle*

How Can I Change Other People Who Are "Professional Victims" . . . Always Blaming Others?

The short answer to that question is: You can't.

The long answer: You can't change anybody but yourself.

The longer answer: You can't change anybody but yourself. But you *may* be able to influence other people—in varying degrees—if you choose to. How do you do that?

First of all, accept people as they are. It sounds like a contradiction, but if you have any hope at all that others may change, you must begin by allowing them NOT to change. Start off by accepting them and making it OK for them to be exactly as they are today.

When people sense that someone is trying to change, fix, or control them, they will instinctively resist. The only way that any of us change is when we are first accepted as we are, and we feel it's OK to change or not, as we choose. Once people feel accepted as they are, then they *may* be open to the possibility of changing—if there's something positive in it for them, and they're inspired by others' examples. They also need to feel assured that others are supporting and helping them, not waiting to criticize, scold, or ridicule them.

Dick Richards, author of *Artful Work,* understands this when he says: "I'm not interested in converting the unconverted. I'm interested in helping the converted become successful." The unconverted will take care of themselves. They'll either see the results that successful people are getting, and they'll get on board, or else they'll die off. Richards works with people who already want to change, who are teachable. He doesn't spend any time at all on those who aren't ready to change.

Related to this notion is the old folk saying: "Never try to teach a pig to sing. It doesn't work, and it only annoys the pig." Don't waste your time and emotional energy by trying to influence someone who clearly isn't interested in taking on personal responsibility.

Some people actually relish the victim role, because they have been in it for so long. They like not having to change, take a risk, or become accountable. Leave them alone; let them wallow in their negativity. And keep your distance from them (without being rude, of course), so that you don't get infected with their "victim virus."

If we hold out the hope that others around us might change and begin to become more responsible, the best thing each of us can do is be superb role models—shining examples of personal responsibility, people who walk their talk. We have to live it ourselves before we can expect anyone else to follow us.

We need to show them how taking initiative and being accountable has led to our professional success and our personal satisfaction. Gandhi said it best: "We must *be* the change we wish to see in the world."

Special note. Whatever you do, avoid finger-wagging and finger-pointing! No one responds well to being scolded or shamed into changing his or her behavior. Don't "should" on people. Instead, influence them through inspiration and example.

Invite them to "experiment" with new ways of approaching their work and their jobs. Experiments are great because they enable people to try out new things on a tentative basis—without feeling they have to make a huge commitment, once and for all. Most people change incrementally, not dramatically. Make it OK for them (and yourself) to take baby steps. Applaud their successes; comfort them when they get discouraged and fall back into old habits; let them know that you're on their side no matter what.

Additional note. Don't spend a lot of time and energy pointing out why being responsible is good for the organization. Far too many people are sick and tired of being told what's in it for the organization. To motivate people, tell them what's in it for *them*! Appeal to them on a personal basis. Show them how taking initiative will help them be successful and happier.

"The man who acts the least,
upbraids the most."

HOMER, *Greek poet, author of the*
Iliad *and the* Odyssey

"What you tell people to *do* often
goes right by them. Who you *are* does not.
The change in you is contagious. When you
yourself change, watch how the people
around you change."

STEVE CHANDLER, *author of*
100 Ways to Motivate Yourself

Imagine a Workplace Where
There Is No "They"...

What if you tried an experiment in your department, work group, or organization—an experiment in which you banned the word "they"? What would that be like?

Consider the Possibility . . .

Team leader: Let's get this meeting started. John, how are things going with your project?

John: OK, but not great. We've run into some problems.

Team leader: Problems? Mary, you're on this project, too—do you concur with John?

Mary nods: Afraid so.

Team leader: John, can you be more specific?

John: Yeah, well, we can't seem to get buy-in from Department X. They just won't get on board.

Team leader: *They?* There is no *they*.

John: Oh yeah, right. Uh, well . . . *we* won't get on board.

Team leader: Why not?

John: I dunno. You'd have to ask them.

Team leader: *Them?*

John: Oh, sorry. You'd have to ask, uh, *us,* I guess—except that *us* isn't here in the meeting.

Team leader: Well, maybe we should get all of *us* here together so we can sort this out.

John: Uh, I guess so.

Mary: That's a good idea. Why don't I call *us* right now and see if some of *us* can be here.

Team leader: OK, and if *us* can't come right now, let's schedule a get-together as quickly as we can, so we can get this resolved.

Mary: Will do.

John: OK.

See the difference that a simple change in language can make? The whole tenor of the discussion changes when there is no longer any "they"—there is only "us" and "we" and "I" and "me."

Try it with your work group . . . just for a week. Try it as an experiment and see what happens. You might even make some buttons or T-shirts like this to remind everyone that "they" no longer exist:

There is only "we." See if it makes a difference for your group. Instead of "us versus them" discussions, try having "us and we" discussions. Language is powerful. Try it and see.

"Your future depends on many things, but mostly yourself."

FRANK TYGER, *oft-quoted philosopher and observer of human behavior*

"The best place to find a helping hand is at the end of your own arm."

ROBERT DEDMAN, *philanthropist, business entrepreneur, and founder of ClubCorp International*

How Accountable and Responsible Are *You?*

Our story demonstrated how easy it is to recognize what others are doing (or not doing), and how hard it is to see *ourselves* clearly. We often have blind spots concerning our own behavior. You can't change your behavior if you're not aware of it. Try to be as self-aware as you can. Be candid and honest in assessing yourself.

On a scale of 1 to 5, circle the number that best describes how accurately each statement describes how you are at work.

1 = never 2 = rarely 3 = sometimes 4 = often 5 = always

1 2 3 4 5   1. When I perceive a problem in my department, I share my concern with my boss and propose suggestion(s) for how to fix the problem.

1 2 3 4 5   2. When I make a mistake, I let my boss and other appropriate people know as quickly as possible. I apologize and do whatever I can to fix my mistake.

1 2 3 4 5   3. When I receive praise, recognition, or a compliment for a job well done, I share the credit with others who helped me in my accomplishment.

1 2 3 4 5   4. When there are problems between my department and another department, I work to pull both groups together to find a "win-win" solution that will help ALL of us.

1 2 3 4 5   5. When I have suggestions for improvement or new ideas that can help my organization be more successful, I share them openly with my boss and/or the appropriate people in my organization.

1 2 3 4 5   6. If I have a problem or misunderstanding with another person in my organization, I go directly to that person to address the problem (rather than complaining to others).

1 2 3 4 5   7. I acknowledge and praise other people who demonstrate their own accountability at work.

1 2 3 4 5   8. I volunteer to take on new, challenging assignments, over and above my regular job.

1 2 3 4 5   9. I think and act proactively, to prevent problems and mistakes and to have contingency plans thought out in case something goes wrong.

1 2 3 4 5   10. When things don't go my way, I try to learn what I can from the situation, make the best of it, and move on. (I don't whine, pout, or hold grudges.)

  _____   **TOTAL SCORE**

SCORING:

HIGH SCORE (40–50): You demonstrate a high level of personal accountability in your own job performance, as well as in your interactions with other people. You know you're not perfect, but you respond in a mature, responsible manner when things go wrong. You're an excellent role model for others in your organization.

MODERATE SCORE (25–39): In some situations, you demonstrate accountability, but sometimes you slip into playing the blame game. Occasionally, you may feel like a victim of other people's decisions or actions.

LOW SCORE (10–24): You prefer to play a more passive role at work—waiting for others to solve problems or improve organizational performance.

"I am only one, but still I am one.
I cannot do everything, but still I can do something.
I will not refuse to do the something I can do."

HELEN KELLER, *author, lecturer, and inspirational role model who overcame severe physical disabilities*

What Do I Gain by Taking Initiative and Assuming Responsibility?

Our story pointed out how frustrated we all feel when we blame others for problems, rather than recognizing problems as opportunities for us to take initiative and *act*. What's in it for us? Plenty!

1. I have more control of my own destiny.
2. I become an active contributor rather than a passive observer.
3. Others look to me for leadership.
4. I gain the reputation as a problem solver.
5. Others are influenced by my positive energy and enjoy working with me.
6. I increase my chances of receiving recognition and enhance my career opportunities.
7. I increase my personal power and influence.
8. I enjoy the satisfaction that comes from getting things done—*the power of positive doing*.
9. I experience less anger, frustration, and helplessness—all of which lead to better physical health.
10. I realize a positive spillover effect into my personal life at home.

ACCOUNTABILITY:
What's in a Word?

Acknowledge the situation.

Courageously face difficulties.

Communicate with positive language.

Own the problem . . . and the solution.

Understand others' viewpoints.

Negotiate solutions that work for everyone.

Take on new responsibilities.

Act, don't simply react.

Be willing to reassess and renegotiate.

Influence others and collaborate.

Leave the "poor me" victim mentality behind.

Initiate thoughtful and deliberate problem solving.

Take pride in your results.

Yes leads to success.

Are You a Whiner or a Winner?

Our parable is a story of transformation. We followed the character on his journey from "whiner" to "winner"—from "victim" to "victor." Ask yourself: *Which one am I?*

WHINERS	WINNERS
Say: "I *should* do X . . . "	Say: "I *want* to do X . . . "
Say: "These people are driving me crazy!"	Say: "I control my own feelings. I'm not going to let these people get to me."
Are focused on what is wrong with others.	Are focused on how they can deal effectively with others.
Think: *How can I get through this?*	Think: *What can I get from this?*
Spend energy reacting.	Spend energy being proactive.
Say: "I'm swamped! I'll never get all this work done!"	Say: "I'm going to prioritize my work and do the most important things first."

WHINERS	WINNERS
Thought patterns and self-talk lead to fatigue and resignation.	Thought patterns and self-talk lead to action.
Complain: "This job is awful."	Assert: "I'm going to have to be very creative to find a way to enjoy this job—or at least not hate it."
Are focused on what is wrong with the situation.	Are focused on what they can *do* in this situation.
Sigh: "I'm so confused, I'll never get the hang of this."	Affirm: "There's a lot here I don't understand. I've got a lot of questions about this. This is going to be a real challenge."
Lament: "I keep making mistakes. I hate this!"	Reframe: "This is harder than I thought. I can see I've still got a lot to learn."
Use language of reaction.	Use language of creation.
Feel powerless. See power and control as being outside themselves.	Feel personal power. See power and control as being inside themselves.

WHINERS	WINNERS
See no choices at all.	See choices in everything.
See only one side of things.	See both sides, or all sides.
Say: "I coulda, woulda, shoulda . . . "	Say: "I did it!"

"Two men in prison looked through bars—one saw mud, the other saw stars."

LANGSTON HUGHES, *poet and novelist, famous for his elucidations of black American life*

Victim No More!

Who wants to be a victim?

Who wants to feel powerless, like someone else is calling the shots?

Most of us *say* we don't want to be victims, but sometimes we *act* like victims anyway. After all, being a victim is easy. I don't have to *do* anything. I don't have to change. There's no extra effort to expend, no risks to take, and no failures to face. I don't have to be responsible for my actions and reactions, and maybe make a mistake. *And,* I get to be self-righteous and morally superior as I criticize others. What a deal!

Obviously, people stay in victim mode because they get something out of it. There's a payoff. They are not bad people—they've simply fallen into the victim role for so long that they don't know any different.

Because we're human, we all occasionally chime in with the "woe is me" lament. Times change and so do organizations. We usually roll with the punches, but sometimes we don't. Occasionally we feel put upon, inconvenienced, frustrated by forces and influences that we don't see and that seem beyond our control. "Poor me." "Why is this happening to me?" "How can 'they' do this to me?" We wallow in self-pity. Or we commiserate with our friends and throw a whole pity party!

But there's a difference between occasionally slipping into victim mentality and spending our entire careers there!

The key point is: It is our *choice.* We can *choose* to dwell on problems, or we can choose to actively pursue positive solutions. Each day, each moment, each situation presents us with those very same choices.

Choosing victimhood doesn't make you bad or wrong—it's simply a way of being. The question is: Does it give you the results you want? Does it work for you? Will it help you achieve the kind of career and life that you dream about? Is it an effective strategy for getting what you really want for yourself and the people you care about? If your answer is "no," all you have to do is *choose differently.* As the old saying goes: "There are no victims, only volunteers."

By simply *noticing* when you have slipped into victim mode, you are afforded the opportunity to *choose.* "Oh, listen to me, I'm whining" or "I'm feeling like a victim here, helpless and hurt." Self-awareness and self-honesty give you the chance to choose differently. "Yuk, I hate this feeling. What can I do to turn this around? How do I make the best of this bad situation?" In short, focus on what you *can* do, not on what you *can't* do.

Becoming a *victor* rather than a *victim* is an ongoing process—it's not a onetime deal. Every day we get to choose again—and again and again. Being a victor instead of a victim is a choice that is always available to me, to you, to all of us. "Victim" is a possible way of being. "Victor" is also a possible way of being. The choice is yours. Choose wisely. It is *your* future that's at stake.

"Anyone who refuses to succumb to the highly contagious Victimis Virus and takes initiative to improve their organization, family, community, or life is a leader. Successful leaders face the same confusing and changing circumstances as everyone else. But a leader doesn't just follow the crowd that drifts down the road of discouragement and mediocrity. Leaders choose where they want to go and then blaze a trail to get there."

JIM CLEMMER, *author, speaker, and business consultant*

When I Own the Problem, I Can Own the Solution

"This is the insight I realized early and return to often: In most situations I am the problem. My mentalities, my pictures, my expectations form the biggest obstacle to my success.

"My effectiveness as a leader and a manager improved dramatically when I learned to see myself as the problem. I learned that when I see performance that is unsatisfactory, the first question to ask is: 'What is it that I did or didn't do that caused that to happen?'

"Understanding that I am the problem allowed me to learn how to become the solution."

—Jim Belasco and Ralph Stayer, *Flight of the Buffalo*

What If I Want to Change?

How can I change myself from whiner to winner, from victimhood to personal responsibility?

How can I become a winner at work?

This may very well be one of the most important questions you ever ask—and good for you for asking it! Raising the question is the first step toward enhancing your sense of personal empowerment and career advancement. But, as the old saying goes, "Watch out for that first step—it's a doozy!"

Wanting to change and do things differently is not optional—it's required. "Ya gotta wanna." Fact is, if people aren't committed to self-improvement, no one or nothing can make them do it. So if you *want* to change, you're off to a good start already—you've got the desire, the motivation, the intent.

So, how can you become a winner at work? The answer is simple, but not easy: practice, practice, practice. Taking charge of your work life and your career success is mostly a matter of learning new behaviors, developing new ways of thinking about yourself and others, and adopting new attitudes about solving problems and achieving goals.

Here are some suggestions to get you going:

- **Watch other people who have what you want, in terms of attitude, behavior, and success, and then follow their lead.** If you want what they have, do what they do. To be a winner at work, hang around the people who already are winners and learn from them. Study, watch, listen, analyze, and practice the positive behaviors you see.

- **Enlist your boss, or someone else you respect, in being your informal coach or your mentor.** Most people love to be asked for their advice, particularly if the request is expressed as a sign of admiration. So, try saying something like: "I'm very interested in becoming more effective in my job, and you're someone whose opinions I respect. Would you be willing to give me some feedback or coaching on an occasional basis? It would mean a lot to me. And it will help me do a better job for the organization." Caution: Be sincere with this. People can sense if you're being phony or simply kissing up!

- **Practice divergent thinking to solve problems.** We are all capable of two kinds of thinking: convergent thinking and divergent thinking. Convergent thinking is the kind we use when we are searching for "*the* one, single, absolute right answer." For example, in math, 1+1 always equals 2.

There are no other possible right answers. Life, however, isn't like math! Rarely is there just one right answer to the problems we encounter. Chances are, there are many possible answers—several of which may be excellent. This is where we want to practice divergent thinking: How many different solutions can we think of for the same problem? Go for quantity in the beginning—brainstorm as many possibilities as you can. Don't worry about evaluating ideas right away, just get them on the table for consideration. Then proceed to sort them out, discuss and evaluate them. Practicing divergent thinking will build your "possibility muscles." You'll get better and better at it over time. You'll begin to be more creative, seeing new possibilities in all kinds of situations!

- **Avoid gossips and negative coworkers as much as you can**—their pessimism and cynicism are contagious. You can quickly get sucked into singing their "ain't it awful" chorus. It is easy to find things to complain about, and it is easier still to find fault with other people—but resist the urge.

- **Of course, sometimes you cannot avoid negative, pessimistic, cynical people.** Perhaps your boss is one of them, or someone on your work team. In these situations, the best you can do is focus on the task at hand, keep your own emotional center and positive attitude, and don't let their negative energy infect you. Sometimes, you can even learn important things from negative people—just take what you can use and leave the rest.

- **There's another reason for avoiding negative coworkers as much as you can: you are judged by the company you keep.** Everyone in your department knows who the effective, successful people are and who the losers are. You don't want to be associated with naysayers, gossips, or poor performers.

- **Watch your language, especially your self-talk.** Language is extremely powerful—it shapes your thinking and colors your feelings. We are often casual, lazy, or even sloppy with our language, underestimating the power of words. As Rudyard Kipling wrote: "Words are the most powerful drug of mankind. Choose them carefully."

- **Listen to yourself as you're talking to people.** What kinds of words do you use? Do you use a "victim vocabulary" or "winner wording"? Words like *problem, hassle, headache, drudge, pain in the butt, boring, stupid, insane, crazy, pointless,* and *frustrating* tend to reinforce negative thinking—our own and others'. If you catch yourself using them, simply stop and correct yourself and instead use other words like *challenge, opportunity, a real stretch, a high goal, the need for creative solutions, resourcefulness, flexibility,* and *can-do attitude.*

- **The phrase "up until now . . . " is a wonderful tool for changing your thinking and attitude— and your behavior as well.** If you catch yourself making negative blanket statements, interrupt that flow of thought, and alter it with: "Up until now . . . " For example, when I hear myself say "I can't do that, I'm no good with computers," I immediately stop and rephrase: "Oh, I mean, up until now, I haven't been good with computers." That opens up the possibility for change and creates a new future that is not determined by my past. "Up until now" reminds me that I can do things differently today—and in the future. "Up until now" gives me freedom to change.

"Have you ever noticed that life is not the way it is supposed to be? It's the way it is. So the way we cope with it is what makes the difference."

VIRGINIA SATIR, *therapist, author, and educator*

Focus on What You *Can* Do,
Not on What You Can't

But be careful you're not fooling yourself about what you *can't* do!

There are undoubtedly many problems in your organization that need attention. The key question to ask is: Which things should you focus on, and which should you ignore or let go? Here's a suggestion: Focus your attention and energy on the things you can do something about, not on the things over which you have no control or influence.

The simplest way to do this is to frequently ask yourself: "Is there something I can do about this problem? In what ways can I contribute to the solution?" Sometimes the answer will be a clear "yes"— and sometimes it will be a clear "no." But be careful, for sometimes that "no" is simply habit, a way of looking at the world that says: "I have no power here—those things are out of my control. I can't change company policies. There's nothing I can do." Maybe so, maybe not.

Perhaps you can do more than you think. Maybe you really *can* do something about things that seem out of your sphere of influence. For instance, you really may be able to influence your organization's policies! If you can point to a policy that is clearly counterproductive, something that does more harm than good, it may be within your power to do your homework, gather data about how the policy is a problem, and what it might be costing the organization in terms of time or money. With this information, you can follow your chain of command to those who made the policy. If your data is solid, and your case persuasive, you may actually be able to influence policy makers into changing the policy!

Better yet, if you do this with a group of coworkers, your case will be even more compelling, and you will all be seen as people who are willing to take initiative and make a difference. If you do this more than once, you will become known as a smart, energetic, and effective change agent. You will be recognized as an informal leader in your organization, and others will respect your newly developed influence skills.

So, think carefully about what you can influence and what you can't—you may be surprised that you have more influence than you think!

"If you think you can, you're right. And if you think you can't, you're right."

MARY KAY ASH, *founder of Mary Kay Cosmetics*

AM I ACCOUNTABLE?

AM I COUNT-ON-ABLE?

Turn Your *Problem* into a Goal by Asking "What Do I Want?"

Got a problem at work? Does it cause you worry and stress? Does it seem like it's someone else's fault? Would you like to trade your worry, stress, and feelings of "poor me" for focus and energy? Here's a very simple and effective tool adapted from Robert Fritz's book, *The Path of Least Resistance.* If you have a problem, the key to solving it is asking yourself this question: "What do I want?"

What you want involves some kind of outcome or result. If you can clarify what you want, then you can turn that into a goal. Where the problem was draining you of energy, having a goal will *give* you energy! This is because solving a problem means trying to make something go away (the problem). But setting a goal is an act of creation; it's positive; it means creating something new. While problem solving generates "push away" energy, goal setting generates "pull toward" energy, which is more positive and pleasant.

Here's how to do it.

First, write down your problem. Don't lump a whole bunch of problems together—just deal with them one at a time. Write it down, whatever it is.

Next, ask yourself: "What do I want?"

Now, take what it is that you want and write it as a goal. Write clearly and specifically what outcome you would like to have, what result you would like to see.

And there you have it! The problem that was troubling you is transformed into a goal toward which you can work.

Here are a couple of examples:

Problem: My boss doesn't tell me what's going on.

Question: What do I want?

Answer: I want to feel in the loop about what's going on.

Goal: I will get information about what's going on in our department.

With this goal in mind, I can create action steps that will lead me to achieving my desired outcome. Perhaps I will develop alternative sources of information to keep myself informed. Perhaps I will set up weekly one-on-one meetings with my boss. Perhaps I will ask my coworkers more questions as a way to keep myself informed.

Problem: I feel stuck and bored in my job, with no chance of advancement.

Question: What do I want?

Answer: I want to be learning on my job and growing in my career.

Goal: I am going to make a career move in the next two years.

Now that I am clear about what I want, I can take steps to get it. I can do research and find out about training classes where I work, and maybe tuition assistance with college courses. I can hire a career coach, or a life coach, to help me explore options. I can update my résumé and look at opportunities in other companies. I can think creatively about all the possible ways to achieve my goal.

Now, try working on one or two of the work problems you're facing:

My problem: _____

Question: What do I want?

My answer: I want _____

My goal: I will _____

My problem: _____

Question: What do I want?

My answer: I want _____

My goal: I will _____

You can use this tool with personal problems, too—for example:

My problem: I am overweight.

Question: What do I want?

My answer: I want to be fit, trim, and healthy.

My goal: I will join Weight Watchers this week and give away 30 pounds by the end of the year.

Try it out on a personal issue that bothers you:

My problem: _____

Question: What do I want?

My answer: I want _____

My goal: I will _____

Problems live in vagueness, in generalized feelings of frustration and anxiety, in a foggy mess that makes you feel bogged down. But goals live in clarity, in the light, with focus. Turning your problems into goals will bring you out of the fog and the bog into clear, focused solutions. Victims and whiners talk about what they *dread* and *fear,* while winners talk about what they *want*!

"I always wondered why somebody didn't do something about that. Then I realized I was somebody."

LILY TOMLIN, *comedienne, actress, and author*

"The problem of distinguishing what we are and what we are not responsible for in this life is one of the greatest problems of human existence. . . . We must possess the willingness and the capacity to suffer continual self-examination."

M. SCOTT PECK, *author of* The Road Less Traveled

Four Stages in Changing Your Outlook, Attitude, and/or Behavior

You didn't develop your personality and your habits overnight—they evolved over many years. So don't expect to change your habits overnight, either. It takes time, repetition, and reinforcement. Be patient with yourself, and acknowledge yourself when you see the progress you're making.

It's best *not* to take on all your character defects at once. Pick one habit at a time and spend several weeks or months working on it. Maybe it's your negative thinking, maybe it's your temper, maybe it's your clutter, or maybe it's your chronic lateness.

Maybe you want to start with small habits you'd like to change—set yourself up for success—then work your way up to tackling some of the bigger things you'd like to change about yourself.

Or maybe you want to try the opposite approach—pick the most troublesome habit you have, the one that would make the biggest difference in your life if you changed it, and work on that one.

It depends on whether you are a "wader" or a "diver"—do you like to wade into things slowly, getting deeper over time, or do you like to dive right into the deep end of things? Either way is just fine. It is completely up to you. There is no right or wrong here, simply a choice. The important thing is that you *begin*—now.

In changing your attitude or something else about yourself, it's helpful to understand how the change process normally works. You will go through four predictable stages or phases.

The first stage is "Unconscious Incompetence": When you are doing something that is not in your own best interest, but you are unconscious of the fact that you are doing it. Perhaps you're acting like a victim and are not even aware of it. It's impossible for you to change at this point, because you don't even know that you need to change!

The second stage is "Conscious Incompetence": You wake up to the fact that you are behaving in a way that is not desirable. Sometimes this is a rude awakening, when the lightbulb goes on in your head, and you say: "Oh my gosh, look what I'm doing!" And you're not happy with what you see: you're whining, complaining, grumbling, blaming, and fault-finding. Sometimes this step is taken when someone else points out your problem behavior, much to your chagrin. It can be embarrassing to have someone draw your attention to your personality or behavior flaws—but you must thank them anyway. He or she has given you the wake-up call that will enable you to see yourself as not acting in your own best interest.

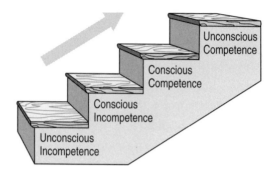

The third stage is "Conscious Competence": When you adopt new behavior in place of the old, but it feels awkward and strange because it is new, and you are acutely conscious of feeling odd about your newly adopted behavior. You practice positive self-talk; you look at every situation and ask: "How can I make the most of this?" You take on the behaviors of a winner, not a whiner. In working to change your attitude, you've essentially put on a new pair of glasses, and you're still very conscious of how different the world looks through these new lenses.

And the final stage to personal change is "Unconscious Competence": The new behavior has become habitual, and you don't have to think about it anymore. It is so routine and part of your normal way of reacting and behaving that it becomes simply part of your unconscious way of being. Your new approach to things is now on solid ground, and you can enjoy the feeling of mastering a new way of being at work.

People who are interested in personal growth and development understand that it's an ongoing process. Just when you've successfully adopted one new behavior or attitude, something else crops up that needs your attention! You discover yet another habit that you want to change. It's all normal. You're a human being who is on a path of self-discovery and self-improvement. You're a work in progress.

"It is never too late to be what you might have been."

GEORGE ELIOT, *English female author (Mary Ann Evans) and philosopher who wrote under a male pen name*

Sometimes the Little Things Can Make a Big Difference . . . (. . . and good practice for taking on bigger things later)

Are you looking for ways to exercise more control at work—to feel happier, more satisfied, more fulfilled? If so, you'll want to start with small things and work your way up to bigger ones. Mark Bryan, author of *The Artist's Way at Work,* suggests not taking on the whole world overnight—don't try to undertake dramatic changes. Instead, focus on lots of little ones. In other words, don't look for one thing that you can do 100 percent better—instead, look for 100 things that you can do 1 percent better.

For instance, look at your workspace. Ask yourself: "What are three simple things I can do to my workspace this week that would make me happier and more effective?"

1. _____

2. _____

3. _____

Now, get into action and do these three things.

Next, focus on your work routines. Ask yourself: "What are three simple things I could do differently in my daily routines this week that would make me happier and more productive?"

1. _____

2. _____

3. _____

Now, get into action and make these three changes.

Next, think about your boss. Ask yourself: "What are three simple things I could do differently in interacting with my boss this week that would make me happier and improve our relationship?"

1. _____

2. _____

3. _____

Now, start interacting differently.

You can do this same simple exercise with other aspects of your work: your interactions with coworkers and teammates, serving customers, dealing with suppliers and vendors, working with technology, and so on. . . .

WHAT ONE THING AM I WILLING

TO DO DIFFERENTLY TODAY

TO MAKE A DIFFERENCE?

The Most Important Words of Personal Responsibility

The 10 most important words:
I won't wait for others to take the first step.

The 9 most important words:
If it is to be, it's up to me.

The 8 most important words:
If not me, who? If not now, when?

The 7 most important words:
Let me take a shot at it.

The 6 most important words:
I will not pass the buck.

The 5 most important words:
You can count on me.

The 4 most important words:
It IS my job!

The 3 most important words:
Just do it!

The 2 most important words:
I will.

The most important word:
Me

"Do more than belong—participate.
Do more than care—help.
Do more than believe—practice.
Do more than be fair—be kind.
Do more than forgive—forget.
Do more than dream—work."

WILLIAM ARTHUR WARD, *author, editor,*
and college administrator

PART THREE

Additional Resources

Training Materials

Please contact:

Peacock Productions
701 Danforth Drive
Los Angeles, CA 90065
Phone 323-227-6205
Fax 323-227-0705
E-mail WhoRTheyAnyway@aol.com
http://www.whoaretheyanyway.com

Who Are "They" Anyway? **Video Training Package**

Based on the story in this book, this animated video is a powerful and effective resource for encouraging personal accountability at all levels in your organization. The complete training package includes a comprehensive *Leader's Guide,* PowerPoint presentation on CD-ROM, participant workbook, and pocket reminder cards.

"The Accountability Quotient™ for Individuals"

This easy-to-use assessment tool is designed for use in conjunction with the *Who Are "They" Anyway?* video to help managers, supervisors, and employees evaluate their own level of personal accountability.

The assessment focuses on five areas of accountability, each affecting your ability to exercise responsibility for your job and career. This is an invaluable tool for anyone interested in increasing their Accountability Quotient™ as a means to enhanced self-confidence, personal fulfillment, and job satisfaction.

"The Accountability Quotient™ for Teams, Work Groups, and Organizations"

This assessment tool is designed to evaluate the culture of accountability within a team, department, work group, or entire organization. Designed for use in conjunction with the video, it can be used with or without the individual assessment. It focuses on five aspects of corporate culture: leadership, performance management, rewards, organizational structure, and accountability to customers. The assessment is simple and straightforward, easy to administer and interpret. Results are used to strengthen accountability throughout your organization.

The Blame Game Video Training Program

If you want to create a work environment where people innovate and try new things, you also need to be prepared for mistakes and problems. Taking risks is part of innovation, and taking responsibility is an essential part of calculated risk taking. This creative, animated video will help show you and your organization who to start finding solutions, rather than blame, when problems occur. Video comes with a *Leader's Guide,* including training designs on "Personal Accountability and Dealing with Change" and "Personal Accountability and Teamwork." Handouts, quizzes, and background material make this a complete training package.

"Count-on-Ability @ Work and in Life" Individual Learning Program

This unique video and workbook package is designed specifically for individuals, rather than groups. Based on the story in this book, the self-study program teaches how to start making positive changes by taking initiative at work and in life. The video is both entertaining and instructive, supplemented with a well-written workbook to help you put the principle of count-on-ability to work in your own life.

For Keynote Speeches, Training,
and Consulting Services
on Taking Initiative
and
Personal Responsibility

Please contact:

Peacock Productions
701 Danforth Drive
Los Angeles, CA 90065

Phone 323-227-6205
Fax 323-227-0705
E-mail WhoRTheyAnyway@aol.com

http://www.whoaretheyanyway.com

About the
Authors

"A woman at peace has stopped looking for someone to blame."

BARBARA JENKINS, *contemporary American writer and observer of human behavior*

"We don't see things as they are, we see things as *we* are."

ANAÏS NIN, *French-born American author and diarist*

"Life is what we make it— always has been, always will be."

GRANDMA MOSES, *American folk artist who lived to be 101*

BJ Gallagher

BJ Gallagher is an accomplished workshop leader and popular speaker specializing in business topics—organizational change, innovation and creativity, workforce diversity, motivation, skills for success—as well as programs for women. She has worked with many corporate clients as well as professional associations, nonprofit groups, and government agencies. Her clients include DaimlerChrysler, IBM, Chevron, Tosco, Nissan, Volkswagen, Baxter Health Care, Phoenix Newspapers Inc., City of Pasadena, U.S. Immigration & Naturalization Service, American Press Institute, John Deere Credit Canada, among others. BJ is a much-in-demand keynote speaker, making frequent presentations at conferences and professional gatherings in the United States, Canada, Latin America, and Europe.

BJ is the coauthor of several business books, including the international bestseller, *A Peacock in the Land of Penguins* (Berrett-Koehler, 2001), which is currently published in 17 languages and sold more than 300,000 copies, and *What Would Buddha Do at Work?* (Ulysses Press and Berrett-Koehler, 2001). She also writes women's books, including *Witty Words from*

Wise Women (Andrews McMeel, 2001) and *Everything I Need to Know I Learned from Other Women* (Conari Press, 2002). Articles about her work have appeared in the *Chicago Tribune,* the *Los Angeles Times,* and *O, the Oprah Magazine.*

Before starting her own business in 1991, she was the manager of training and development for the *Los Angeles Times,* where she had key responsibilities in the areas of high-potential leadership development, management and supervisory training, workforce diversity, team building, career development, sales training, and customer relations. Prior to that, she was the director of staff training and professional development for the University of Southern California, where she directed numerous programs for both faculty and staff.

BJ is a Phi Beta Kappa graduate of USC, having earned her bachelor's degree summa cum laude in the field of sociology. She has completed the course work for a Ph.D. in social ethics, also at USC. She is an active member of the National Association of Women Business Owners, the National Speakers Association, the American Society of Training and Development, and PEN Center USA West.

Contact her at 701 Danforth Drive, Los Angeles, CA 90065; phone 323-227-6205, fax 323-227-0705; e-mail bbjjgallagher@aol.com.

Steve Ventura

Steve Ventura is a recognized and respected author, graphic artist, book producer, educator, and award-winning training program designer. His work reflects more than 25 years of human resources development experience—as both a practitioner and a consultant—and more than ten years in law enforcement.

As a consultant and trainer, he has had the opportunity to work with scores of notable organizations, including AT&T, General Electric, Shell Oil, Allied-Signal Aerospace, General Dynamics, PacBell, AMD, Northwest Airlines, Texaco, ExxonMobil, and Texas Utilities. His areas of expertise include management, leadership, communication, customer service, and performance improvement.

Before starting his own business in 2002, he was vice president of product development for the Walk the Talk® Company in Dallas, Texas. Prior to that, he was a police officer for the City of Berkeley, California, before accepting the position of manager of operations training for the Bay Area Rapid Transit District.

He has a bachelor's degree in art and mass communication from California State University, and a master's degree in public administration from the University of San Francisco. He has published articles in trade journals such as *Training, Training & Development,* and *Food & Service* magazine. He is coauthor of the popular handbooks *Walk Awhile in My Shoes* (more than 750,000 copies sold) and *Forget for Success,* and has written, edited, and produced 15 other highly successful business publications.

Contact Steve at ventura@airmail.net or 972-317-6380.

"We have a Bill of Rights.
What we need is a
Bill of Responsibilities."

BILL MAHER, *comedian, social critic, and media personality*

"Being responsible sometimes
means pissing people off."

GENERAL COLIN POWELL, *U.S. Secretary of State and former Chairman of the Joint Chiefs of Staff*

Acknowledgments

Many people played a role in bringing our book into the world, in helping us take it through all the stages—from idea to proposal, to manuscript, to revisions, to the volume you now hold in your hands. This finished product has been seen by many eyes, influenced by many minds, shaped by many voices, and nourished by many hearts. We are deeply grateful.

Cindy Zigmund and Jon Malysiak welcomed us to our new publishing partnership with Dearborn Trade Publishing, and we have enjoyed getting to know the entire creative team that works there. Thank you one and all. It's been a great collaboration! Joel Marks was the matchmaker who brought us together with Dearborn—he's a fine *yenta*, indeed!

Our professional friends and colleagues were invaluable in their editorial feedback and critiques of early versions of the book. Among them are Ken Blanchard, Dana Kyle, Martha Lawrence, Simon Li, Joan Hill, Ann Marsh, Leslie Yerkes, Charles Decker, Warren Schmidt, Joel Marks, Bill Sheridan, Anita Goldstein, Paul Schneider, Joel Suzuki, Joel Leskowitz, John Denney, and Marilyn Jensen. Many, many thanks to all of you! Your love and support made our writing journey a wonderful experience.

Thanks to our families and friends who understood when we said, "Not now, I'm on deadline." Their understanding and patience enabled us to concentrate on the task at hand—knowing that they would be waiting for us when we came up for air. Our love for them cannot possibly be described in words.

And, finally, we bow our heads humbly and quietly, in a simple prayer of thanks to the Divine Source of all creativity . . . and responsibility.

"I think the purpose of life is to be useful, to be responsible, to be honorable, to be compassionate. It is, after all, to matter: to count, to stand for something, to have made some difference that you lived at all."

LEO C. ROSTEN, *American writer, scholar, and humorist*